SILENT SKY

WORDS FROM THE LIFE OF A TEEN THROUGH POETRY

ALIYA ABUBAKAR BASRAVI

ISBN 979-888569860-3

Contents

Contents

Contents

Contents

Preface

My name is Aliya Abubakar Basravi, a fifteen year old girl who loves and enjoys writing. As a first time young poetess, I have decided to publish my first ever own collection of quotes and poems. I believe poetry can be a savior of the heart. It's such a thing where the soul cries through words. A human heart feels a lot of emotions and few express them by saying it out loud and some choose to be quiet while others find writing as their listener. I wrote this book in the hope that the readers may find themselves in the words I wrote and believe that they are not alone suffering. I believe that it's the little things that matter the most. This book contains words related to everyday kinds of emotions and the little feelings which matter. I hope you find this book easy to read and appreciatable.

This book contains lovely quotes (poetic words) and some poems. I hope the reader can enjoy this simple book and can leave their beautiful review.

And also can follow on:

Instagram: @arbitrary_us

Twitter: @aliya_basravi

QUOTES

1. DAY DREAM

"Day Dreaming is just like building castles in the air and at a blink of an eye everything disappears."

2. BOND

"Our bond is nothing but an incomplete melody that needs more lyrics to make it a complete story."

3. SOUL

• 3 •

"It was her heart that shined the brightest and the one which covered her scattered soul."

4. TRUTH

*"The more we know the reality of life,
the more easier it is to accept the truth."*

5. FUTURE

• 5 •

"*Just as a star needs a dark sky to shine,*

so as your life needs a dark past for a bright future."

6. UNUSUAL

• 6 •

"There's always something unusual with the silence of a joyful heart."

7. COURAGE

•7•

"*People who are on the way to rebuild themselves have most of the courage*
to live again in this nasty world."

8. ALIVE

• 8 •

"All I know is we need what we want.
And if we didn't get what we want,
we will lose all that hopes which kept us alive."

9. PURPOSE

• 9 •

*"I have come to a point that no one actually cares for you.
They be with you just for their own purpose."*

10. KIND

• 10 •

"And all in the end, it's just you with you.
So be kind to yourself first."

11. GROWTH

"*You grow when you learn to get out of your own sorrows.*"

12. HAPPINESS

"If it is happiness, take it with you.
And if it is sadness,
wrap it in a baggage and leave it behind."

13. HOPE

• 13 •

"Things are full of hopes even when you feel hopeless."

14. LOVE PAIN

• 14 •

"Try to kiss your pain.
It will love you back the way you loved it."

15. WORTH

"*The time she knew her worth,
she doesn't have to wait for anyone to tell her.*"

16. FREE

• 16 •

"When you allow yourself to overcome all of your fears,
you free your soul and make it comfortable to live in this world."

17. CHAOS

"She sang her chaos to the world in such a way that everyone loves to listen it every day."

18. TIME

• 18 •

"Time says a lot in seconds."

19. SCRIBBLED

• 19 •

"The more you get scribbled by your thoughts, the more beautifully you can describe the pain."

20. ROME

"She was more than just a human,
a soul who reminded me of Rome."

21. BLANKET

• 21 •

"All she wants is your love as a blanket to her soul."

22. SHE

• 22 •

"She just made me feel more like home, when my own people left me homeless."

23. LITTLE

• 23 •

"She cares because she knows the pain the little shoulders hold."

24. CHANGE

"*Time goes on and on. But some things never change. That's not because time didn't let it, it's because we didn't allowed it to do so.*"

25. ASHAMED

"Some people love you but they hate you just because others hate you. They won't show their love because they are too ashamed to be odd in front of others."

26. LEARN

• 26 •

"In every pain there is more to learn and less to be sad of."

27. GREED

• 27 •

"*There's so much a heart could be thankful for, but it's the human mind not allowing it to do so and the one which makes the soul greedier.*"

28. BEAST

• 28 •

"The beast was not a beast and only beauty believed it."

29. CENTURY

• 29 •

"She owns such a world that could even take centuries to find for but you can't find one."

30. TORN SOUL

• 30 •

"She stitched her own torn soul and rebuilt herself in such a way that no one could ever thought of."

31. WAVES

"*I have been fooled by the waves that promised me
to help me see the sight of the shore.*"

32. CARVED

"*She carved for the spark that set her on fire.*
And it was nothing but a kind heart."

33. PRETTY, SILLY

• 33 •

"We are all perfect in those pretty pictures, silent cries, silly smiles and sleepless nights."

34. HEAL

• 34 •

"You heal when you conquer the little monsters inside."

35. ONCE

"Even if it's for once upon a time, my heart will still beat for you."

36. OUNCE

• 36 •

"It took every ounce of me to forget the pain solemnly."

37. THIN

• 37 •

"I am living in all those thin scribbled lines which are near to break everytime you try to touch it."

38. INSECURE

• 38 •

"I am still finding a place to hide all of my insecurities."

39. TASTE

• 39 •

"It's necessary for the rain to fall if you want to taste the sun."

40. SKIP

"Her beauty is worth making my heart skip a beat."

41. STORM

"*You know your worth when you are torn by the storm.*"

42. SHEILD

• 42 •

"*Her body wore all the scars as a shield for the soul to be happy and free.*"

43. DESIRE, CHANGE

• 43 •

"It's our own desires that kill us the most."

"Change is bitter, but necessary."

POEMS

POEMS

44. BE YOURSELF

• 47 •

With all the bruises in her heart,
wearing all her flaws and her scars.
A little perfect and a little imperfect.
Yet standing bright and tall.
Yelling at the world,
yes this is me,
at least not the one who you wanted me to be.

45. FAITH AND ME

People are always in doubt
by seeing me standing tall
during my hardest storm.
Little do they know that
I'm not one one of them who fall
and never will they know
the relationship between me and my lord.

46. COLLAPSED PILLER

Her world was nothing
but a faded fantasy
in which souls collapsed
and things were constantly bombarded.

47. MAKE-BELIEVE

• 50 •

In a world of make-believe,
things flow like a stream.
As it flows through the depths and
passes through the highs,
it learns to adjust itself between
the fearful falls and again to move on.

48. SHINE WITHIN

There's a time when you're broken down,
teared by all,
criticized for who you are.
And you know what's the best thing in return is
to shine from within without bothering them anymore.

49. HER SILENCE

Her woes and words were not bothered.
So, she learned to live in the dark
and that's when her world started to make noise.

50. REPLENISH SOUL

• 53 •

Faded dreams,
lost hopes,
broken hearts,
scattered souls.
When you replenish it ,
you enter a whole new version of yourself.

51. MY HOME, HER SOUL

She was all that you need and adore for.
On your darkest days and nights and overwhelmed mornings.
She reminded you that your not lost, your just right there where you needed to be
HOME.

52. UNWANTED GARDEN

Pull out the weeds from your life.
They are just other beings that
live in your life fighting for shelter
and space and release their toxins in return.
They make your garden look beautiful
but meaningless.

53. A GROWTH OF NEW CHAPTER

I stood there still.
Like a tree,
hoping that all the heavy
droplets
of sorrow would fall off
leaf by leaf,
and vow to start a new chapter of growth,
in a new place,
with fresh soil and mud,
and sow my seeds in a happy orchard,
and enjoy the company of other evergreen trees.

54. MY HEART FOR YOU

• 57 •

I carved a bed
in my heart,
out of blood, pain,
love and flesh
for you to lay inside
peacefully,
away from all those worlds wildness.

55. BEAT

Even if it's for once upon a time,
my heart will still beat for you.

56. TOXIC POSITIVENESS

• 59 •

Her heart was full of love and hope,
and it was the only thing that killed her soul.

57. MY WOLVES INSIDE

I'm alive,
hiding out in the
dark thick woods.
Wolves accompany me.
Every night,
I sit with them,
howling to the moon,
singing to the stars,
climbing the mountains,
and standing at its peaks.
Seeing the sun rising
and me standing proud.

58. SEE-SAW LOVE

You lighted my heart
with so many beautiful lies.
And now that it's all over,
will you ever come back
again? To fill
my heart with forever.
And this time for real?

59. HOPELESS HOPE

I was there,
standing still
looking at you,
wearing that beautiful smile,
warmth in your eyes.
And at that time,
I realized that I wasn't
really good enough for you
and glad that you got what
you deserve.

60. WAS IT EVEN FOR REAL

Motionless,
stupefied,
or what else should I say,
hoping this all
was just a dream.
I really cared,
but you didn't realize
and left me in these chains.
I tried harder and harder
but couldn't escape.
With hope in my eye,
weary days,
still waiting for you to come back,
but I was wrong.
My love,
is this the ending you have promised me for?

61. THE MOON

I was lost
then I found the moon,
shining in all that dark,
surrounded by stars.
He's the only one odd out there,
but still spreads its wings.
He's the perfect example
for us to know,
that it's okay to be on our own.
He might be different,
but still loved by all.
He also makes the falling stars
look beautiful in that
silent sky.

62. FRESH WITH MEMORIES

We all paint pictures of people
in our mind.
Some paintings are messed up,
colours spilled,
few dark and some thin,
story closed as a past.
But we still hold some
special place for some people in our lives,
who actually make a difference to us.
We store them in a secured place,
brightly painted,
neat and clean
and fresh with memories.

63. LIGHT AND DARK

We all gaze at the sky,
don't we?
At least for once in our lives.
The constellation of stars,
beautifully formed,
the quite cold winds
passing through you,
reflecting back on fun
and peaceful memories.
But we can learn one thing more,
it is that
no matter how much
you are surrounded by darkness,
you still can shine
and change the whole view.

64. ETERNITY FIGHTS

We all are broken inside.
There's a part of us
pushing in that dark,
again and again.
But we still rise,
still fight and try and try,
until we release ourselves
from that capture.

65. FADE

You're standing in the rain
trying to fade away.
Taking every chance of life
to be happy.
Cause you know,
the same moment won't come
again and again.

66. A DOOR UNOPENED

The answer was there itself.
It was there.
You've simply taken your
whole life trying to figure it out
in all the possible ways,
but left that door.
Because you know that
you won't be able to
accept the truth.
So, you have allowed yourself
to be in these walls of lies,
so you could bring at least
some more peace
to your heart.

67. UNIVERSE IN HER

And there between those
eyes and smile,
lived something
which was
unknown to the universe.
It was magical.
As I tried harder
and harder
to look deep inside,
I only lost myself more
and couldn't come back
home.

68. LETTING IT GO

It's not always about
giving up.
Nope it's not.
Sometimes it's just that
we feel too much about
something that we couldn't hold on
much longer to it.
So, we finally let it go,
for the sake of some
peace.

69. ENDLESS TOGETHER

Will you climb
the mountains of life
with me
both together,
for each other.
Holding hands,
silent sky,
cold winds?
No matter what we
pass through
fighting back together.
Loving each other harder,
laughing and crying,
sleepless nights?
Are you ready for these,
just both of us?
Living the life
that we meant to have.

70. TOUCH OF LOVE

Soft
whispers
that come
from your soul
are pure enough
to make my heart warm.

71. EVERLASTING

You are my favorite
song to dance on.
You're my favorite
lipstick colour.
A perfect summer.
Few sunsets,
slow music and jolly souls.

72. STITCHED SOUL

• 75 •

Night falls
and I cried again.
Heart turned to ashes
and I wasn't able to stick again.

73. HOLD ON AWHILE

My soul finds ease
whenever I be with you.
It cries every time,
thinking of all the moments
made together.
I know that
you're all gone now
but I still wish (that)
I should have hold onto you
a little more
and never allowed
you to go.

74. HUMAN

We humans,
a man of flesh and blood.
More than just skin.
Swarmed with jealousy, love,
hate.
Few fulfill their dreams
and few chicken out,
just because of their
fear of failure.
Oh man!
When will you understand?
This life is a series of
ups and downs.

75. MY SAVIOUR

My love,
I have broken
your heart many times.
But even after this
I like the way you
fix them and come back
to save mine.

76. FLAMEING

The spirit you hold
is a flame.
With your every touch
my skin burns
and my soul turns to ashes.
Sometimes I sit down
and think,
how can someone
be so pure enough
that even death
feels beautiful
when killed by them.

Author Introduction:

Aliya Abubakar Basravi (shortly known as Aliya Basravi), is a fifteen year old girl living in India. She started sharing her words through instagram and it has been two years. Inspired by many great writers, she wrote her first poem when she was in fifth grade. Ever since then her passion for writing increased and she had been writing till now.

A poet or poetess doesn't always need a past to write beautiful stuff. Some simply get inspired and dig deep on a topic. Their minds open up to a whole new aspect and they try to feel every emotion from every individual's eye. Aliya Basravi is also one such poetess.

You can read her writings on the following platforms:

INSTAGRAM: @arbitrary_us

TWITTER: @aliya_basravi

www.ingramcontent.com/pod-product-compliance
Lightning Source LLC
Chambersburg PA
CBHW052147150726
48002CB00003B/1078